Funeral and Memorial Meetings

First published in May 1998 by
QUAKER HOME SERVICE,
Friends House,
Euston Road,
London NW1 2BJ.

All rights reserved. No part of this book may be reproduced or transmitted in any form or by any means, electronic or mechanical, including photocopy, without permission in writing from Quaker Home Service. Reviewers may quote brief passages.

Copyright © Committee on Eldership & Oversight 1998

ISBN 0-85245-301-9

Printed in Friends House, London
filename: QHS\E&O2.pm5

CONTENTS

1 INTRODUCTION 4

2 RESPONSIBILITY AND DELEGATION 5

3 THINKING AHEAD TO ONE'S OWN FUNERAL 6

4 PRELIMINARY PLANNING OF FUNERAL 9

5 DETAILED PLANNING OF FUNERAL 10

6 PLANNING OF THE MEETING FOR WORSHIP 11

7 DUTIES ON THE DAY 13

8 INTRODUCING AND CLOSING THE MEETING 14

9 TASKS AFTERWARDS 16

10 THE DIRECT EXPERIENCE OF FRIENDS & MEETINGS 17

FUNERALS & MEMORIALS FORM - guidance and 18-19
information in advance ✳

10 THE DIRECT EXPERIENCE OF FRIENDS & MEETINGS 20
(continued)

TABLE 1 - PRELIMINARY PLANNING 25

TABLE 2 - DETAILED PLANNING 26

PUBLICATIONS 27

ORGANISATIONS 32

✳ This form can be photocopied, or adapted, according to local meeting practice. Sensitivity is needed when handing out the form or advertising its availability. The meeting should make clear which Friends (at least two) should be given the filled-in forms. When Friends move, an opportunity should be offered to revise it with the aim of forwarding it to the next meeting.

1 - INTRODUCTION

Friends should come to a funeral with both heart and mind prepared. We want to experience a deep sense of communion with God and with one another, which we hope will comfort and strengthen those who mourn. There are at least two aims in our worship: to give thanks to God for the life that has been lived, and to help the mourners to feel a deep sense of God's presence.

Hardshaw East Monthly Meeting Elders & Overseers, 1986,
Quaker faith & practice 17.01

1.1 If the heart and the mind are to be free to worship, mourn and comfort, then all the organisation of a Quaker funeral or memorial meeting has to be sensitive, prayerful, efficient and unobtrusive. There is so much to remember and do, yet time is short. Each funeral and each memorial meeting will need to be planned individually, the organisers have to be flexible, yet there are certain legal, practical and Quaker requirements.

1.2 *Funerals and memorial meetings* brings together the experience and advice of over eighty Friends and meetings, to amplify and complement chapter 17 of our book of Christian discipline, *Quaker faith & practice*. The Committee on Eldership & Oversight is most grateful to all those who have contributed, sharing their experience with others in Britain Yearly Meeting. We hope that this booklet in the eldership and oversight handbook series will help readers not only to respond appropriately when a death occurs but also to make sensible preparations.

1.3 This booklet is addressed primarily to funeral coordinators in Quaker meetings, and to all those responsible for oversight and eldership, whether specifically appointed or not. The next of kin and those who are taking thought for their own deaths will find this a useful booklet, too. Funeral directors and the staff at a crematorium or cemetery may also find this booklet helpful when working with Quaker clients.

1.4 Throughout the book we have assumed that a funeral or memorial meeting, with a meeting for worship after the manner of Friends, and under the care of the meeting, is being planned. A Quaker funeral or memorial meeting may be organised for a member or attender, or sometimes it is the mourners who are most closely linked to Friends. However this booklet may also be of use when Friends experienced in organising such gatherings are asked to help with a religious but non-denominational funeral (the meeting not being formally involved); they may be glad to give this service. All concerned need to be agreed what kind of event is being planned.

1.5 The preparation for a funeral is in many ways similar to that for a memorial meeting, and the practicalities often overlap. There is no rigid distinction between the two in this booklet, and the terms are sometimes interchangeable.

1.6 A good funeral may be our last service to the one who died, and a precious gift to those who grieve. It makes demands on each of us, and is not a light task, yet it can be one of the most rewarding of our duties. An elder wrote, 'I was given the strength at that time; it was a real gift of grace in answer to my prayers. I was able to do what I was required to, with the dignity and composure that is *not* my wont. I have never forgotten the experience. *Quaker faith & practice* 26.04, in the words that Caroline Fox heard, says "Live up to the light thou hast and more will be granted thee." Truly God speaks...'

2 - RESPONSIBILITY AND DELEGATION

2.1 This volume of the handbook series on eldership and oversight is concerned principally with offering information and advice to elders, overseers and those responsible for oversight and eldership where the tasks are shared. The essential guidance given in chapter 17 of *Quaker faith & practice* is elaborated in this booklet. We have included a form which could be deposited with the meeting, indicating the wishes of the living about the manner of their funerals: see pages 18-19.

2.2 When someone dies it is important that loving support and sympathy are offered to the bereaved. It is equally important to offer practical help, for any death results in a chain of practical actions with which the bereaved may be unable to cope unaided. Burial in a Quaker burial ground may be requested. The funeral or memorial meeting may be under the care of a Quaker Meeting.

2.3 The person ultimately responsible for decisions and for the costs of the funeral may be a spouse, partner, parent, sibling, child, close friend or relative, colleague, neighbour, executor or solicitor. We have used various terms for this person, most often *next of kin*. When a death occurs, it may not be immediately clear who this responsible person is, and sensitivity is needed in liaising with those close to the deceased.

2.4 Monthly meetings, according to *Quaker faith & practice* 17.07, are responsible but for practical reasons usually delegate responsibilities. *Quaker faith & practice* 12.12.f gives the responsibility for the meeting for worship on a special occasion to elders - perhaps specially appointed for the occasion. Section 12.12.q reminds overseers of the duty to respond to the needs of the bereaved. Delegation may be to monthly meeting elders as a whole, or to overseers, to a sub-committee of those responsible for oversight and eldership, or to a funeral arrangements committee or burial ground committee constituted in some other way. Delegation may be on a preparative meeting basis. In some meetings the Registering Officer for marriages is asked to be responsible for funerals also.

2.5 The method by which such Friends are appointed should be kept under review, and the members of the meeting should be regularly notified of the names of those Friends appointed to carry out these responsibilities - see *Quaker faith & practice* 17.08. In the interests of simplicity we refer to the appointed individual or group in this booklet as the *funeral coordinator*. The Committee on Eldership & Oversight, in using this term, is not recommending any particular practice or terminology.

2.6 There is no one correct way for a monthly meeting to carry through such delegation. What is essential, however, is that the agreed procedures within each monthly meeting are both clearly understood and faithfully followed, for there is a wide range of tasks to be undertaken speedily, together with others that may be appropriate in certain circumstances. Sensitivity and flexibility are needed in carrying out these tasks, but clarity of responsibility will always be essential. Perhaps the first task of elders and overseers is to ensure that the delegation of a monthly meeting's responsibilities for funerals is thoroughly understood by Friends within that meeting.

3 - THINKING AHEAD TO ONE'S OWN FUNERAL

3.1 It is advisable that all Friends consider in life certain material issues that will be consequent upon their death, as *Quaker faith & practice* 4.19 reminds us. Notable among them are the making of a will, the preferred method for the disposal of the body, and the form of remembrance that seems personally preferable. Each of these items is dealt with in turn below. To formalise these personal choices, and to make them readily available to the funeral coordinator, Friends should be encouraged to make them known in advance to the funeral coordinator, solicitor, next of kin, or preparative meeting clerk, as appropriate. (Remember that a will is sometimes not read until after the funeral is arranged). A photocopiable form for such advance planning is on pages 18-19. The role of those responsible for oversight and eldership in these matters is to encourage Friends to make such choices and to ensure that the meeting is aware of their wishes. By so doing they will facilitate the ultimate funeral arrangements, and the bereaved will be helped to make the decisions that will inevitably be painful to face immediately after a death.

3.2 Because of life's uncertainties Friends have always recognised that wills should be made in times of health and strength of judgment so as to prevent the inconvenience, loss and trouble that their dying intestate may cause to relatives and friends. Apart from financial bequests, there are other points to be covered that are relevant to organising the funeral or memorial meeting. In particular any special wishes for the disposal of one's body should be indicated in one's will, though this should be supported by further specific actions. It is also helpful to indicate that any funeral is to be conducted after the manner of Friends: this applies equally to the wills of non-Quakers who so desire, so that the request can be considered promptly. The will, therefore, needs to be read before the funeral is arranged. Those likely to plan the funeral need to know where the will is kept.

3.3 However, it may not be possible for practical reasons to carry out precisely all the wishes of the deceased. Also, the first priority is to support those who are grieving: the needs of the bereaved may have to take precedence over the wishes of someone now dead.

3.4 Foremost for consideration is the preferred method of disposal of one's body. There are four main methods.

3.4.1 Burial is not as easy to arrange as it once was. Where a Quaker burial ground is available, any wish to be buried there needs to be noted. *Quaker faith & practice* 17.11-13 should be consulted. Where the use of a local churchyard or cemetery is contemplated, prior consultation with and the agreement of the appropriate authorities are desirable. Alternatively, burial may be on privately owned land: the owner's permission should be sought (see *What to do when someone dies* and *New Natural Death Handbook* for this and other detailed information: 'Publications List', page 27).

3.4.2 Cremations, because they involve the use of publicly owned facilities, demand little in the way of prior agreement, and arrangements will largely be finalised only after death. However, the wish for cremation and for the place of disposal of the ashes should be covered in the will, and the wish made known to the meeting before death (see 3.1 above).

3.4.3 'Green' burials involve the same actions as do traditional burials but facilities vary round the country, so they may take a little more time to research and organise (see 'Publications list', page 27, and 'Organisations', page 32).

3.4.4 Gifts of bodies or organs for medical research are becoming increasingly common. Arrangements must be made in advance with the appropriate medical authorities, and details included within the will and/or in the form deposited with the meeting. It should be borne in mind that a body may not be accepted for medical purposes and may be returned to the bereaved: furthermore the remains may be returned for burial or cremation after their medical usefulness has been exhausted. For both these reasons, any will that includes this option should choose a second method of disposal to accommodate these circumstances.

3.5 The Quaker belief in that of God in every one and our resulting testimony on equality can be seen in the plainness of our burial grounds and the uniformity of any stones - see *Quaker faith & practice* 15.20, also 20.27-36. Simplicity is another testimony which would influence how we plan the funeral. Our reverence for life and concern for the integrity of creation would encourage Friends to find out about 'green' burials and biodegradable coffins. Costs can be very high, and need to be borne in mind, as the following 1998 examples show. An ecological coffin can be purchased for under £100. Nonetheless, the cost of the coffin, the funeral directors' charges and the fees for the crematorium are rarely less than £1100. A burial is usually £100 to £200 more expensive, plus the cost of any memorial. Burial in London and other major cities can be much more expensive. Most funeral directors (the term 'undertaker' is seldom used now) offer only a 'package' funeral, and it may be difficult to obtain a simple bespoke funeral. Funeral directors who will provide simple, inexpensive funerals are listed by The Natural Death Centre (see page 33). Although codes of practice and charters should ensure that those organising a funeral are given full information, including fees and the provision of a simple funeral if wanted, it can be hard for those recently bereaved to take in all the information and make an unhurried choice.

3.6 The preferred form of remembrance may be an issue that concerns some people. The choice includes: an entirely private funeral, with or without a meeting for worship, organised by those close to the deceased; a meeting for memorial or thanksgiving under the care of the Quaker meeting before, at, following, or entirely separate from the burial or cremation; a simple remembrance by Friends in the meeting for worship on the following Sunday. The wish for any one of these need not, of course, preclude the possibility that a second option may also be implemented, maybe at a later date.

4 - PRELIMINARY PLANNING OF FUNERAL

4.1 There are certain necessary actions consequent upon a death within a meeting that need to be taken immediately. *What to do when someone dies* and similar books (see 'Publications list', page 27) give comprehensive guidance on legal and other requirements in England, Wales and Scotland. In this booklet we concentrate on the Quaker aspects.

4.2 Whoever hears of such a death should inform the funeral coordinator who should then ensure that the following actions are taken by Friends within the meeting, some of whom will have already been appointed for such purposes and some of whom will need to be selected on a personal basis by the funeral coordinator:

- offers of condolences to the bereaved
- giving of practical help as necessary to the bereaved, including help in
- notifying relatives, friends and Quakers
- helping the bereaved with funeral arrangements

4.3 The funeral coordinator, knowing the wishes of the deceased as deposited with the meeting (see pages 18-19), should then arrange a meeting with the next of kin or those charged with making funeral arrangements. It may be advantageous for the funeral director to be present at this meeting. The matters to be discussed and agreed are also summarised in Table 1, on page 25.

4.4 There may be a problem if the deceased had little connection with the meeting, or the next of kin know nothing about Quaker ways. It would be wise to check what is possible or appropriate, before any discussion with the spouse, partner or other appropriate person. For example, if the Quaker burial ground is small, space may be limited to those with a close connection with the meeting. If use of the Quaker burial ground is not possible, there could be a funeral elsewhere under the care of the meeting, or a private event can be arranged with the support and advice of the funeral coordinator.

4.5 Some mourners at the funeral may need special consideration when planning, for example those travelling from abroad, those who are house-bound or disabled in one way or another, children and young people who may attend for only part of the funeral or need care elsewhere. Their needs and wishes may not be obvious: as far as possible, they should be consulted directly.

5 - DETAILED PLANNING OF FUNERAL

5.1 The actions following the first meeting with the next of kin and/or funeral director lead imperceptibly into detailed planning of the funeral. Further meetings may be necessary with close family and friends, and will be essential with the supervisor of the crematorium or cemetery.

5.2 If a Quaker burial ground is to be used the funeral coordinator should notify or meet with the monthly meeting Friend authorised to issue orders for burial or the scattering and interment of ashes, and find out the local procedures. Monthly meeting elders should be notified if a non-member has expressed a wish for a funeral held in the manner of Friends.

5.3 Where a crematorium or a cemetery is to be used, it is essential for the funeral coordinator to meet with the staff and supervisors; this meeting may also involve the next of kin and the funeral director. The following matters should be resolved:

5.3.1 details of time and timing of funeral should be agreed; it may be necessary to arrange a suitable compromise, particularly since only 15-20 minutes may be allowed for a service in a crematorium (it may be possible to book a double session)

5.3.2 at a burial the location of the grave should be visited and the availability of diggers confirmed

5.3.3 the procedures at a crematorium governing the curtains, music, microphone and loop-system should be understood

5.3.4 the seating arrangements should be inspected and, if possible, amended to meet any anticipated special need

5.3.5 if there are any religious symbols considered to be undesirable, it should be established whether they can be moved or covered

5.3.6 the funeral director and supervisor should be made fully aware of the way in which the funeral will be conducted, including the silences, and the manner in which it should be closed

5.3.7 the funeral director and the next of kin should be made aware that there is no Quaker equivalent to a minister's fee; if, however, contributions are made, their distribution should be agreed in advance

5.3.8 if there is to be a collection, its distribution should be settled in advance.

5.4 At this same meeting, the funeral coordinator should check parking arrangements and public transport facilities. Toilet facilities should be noted, and wheelchair access explored.

6 - PLANNING OF THE MEETING FOR WORSHIP

6.1 Planning of the details of the meeting for worship, and indeed any memorial meeting, will overlap with the funeral details, and the whole process will in practice form a continuum. All programmed items should be settled in advance by the funeral coordinator, see *Quaker faith & practice* 17.04 and 17.09. They may include readings, prayers, music, tapes and prepared ministry: in each case the individuals concerned should be aware of the desirable timing of their contributions. Friends may choose to produce leaflets of information to be handed to all who attend the funeral: these may include details of the manner of Quaker worship, and practical information about arrangements such as hospitality after the funeral. Such leaflets should be prepared and obtained before the meeting for worship. Similarly, if a leaflet for remembrance is to be distributed it should be prepared and printed in good time. Such leaflets help the family take an active part in planning the event; they are something to look at if the silence is found difficult; they provide memories of the occasion and can be sent to people unable to be present. Short personal reminiscences of the deceased can be included in the leaflets, as can appropriate Quaker or other quotations. Finally, public notices of the memorial meeting should be drafted, agreed with the next of kin and placed with the press and in *The Friend* as requested.

6.2 Where a meeting for worship is held at a crematorium the order of entry must be decided in advance (coffin, mourners, family) as must the provision of a stand for the coffin. Towards the end of the meeting, the timing of the removal of the coffin and the drawing of any curtains need to be agreed. The doors should be opened for the worshippers to leave after the shaking of hands, not after the curtains are drawn. Funeral directors and crematorium staff need to be kept informed where Quaker practice differs from other kinds of funeral.

6.3 Where a meeting for worship is held at a graveside or at a chapel attached to the cemetery, the order of arrival must be decided as must arrangements for and timing of the lowering and covering of the coffin. Access to the graveside may be particularly difficult for the chair-bound and infirm, and it may be helpful to provide garden chairs.

6.4 If a meeting for worship is to be held separately from the funeral its location must be agreed, whether at the home of the deceased or of a relative, at a meeting house, at a church or chapel, or at some other venue. So must its timing, which could be before disposal, when the coffin may or may not be present, immediately after disposal, or at some later date.

6.5 Wherever the meeting for worship is held the funeral coordinator will need to ensure that individual Friends agree to help. The Friends who will act as elders must undertake to be present and should decide amongst themselves who will open and close the meeting, explain what will happen to those unaccustomed to Quaker meetings, and make any necessary announcements. Doorkeepers should be agreed upon, and it should be ensured that enough Friends are available to keep the meeting. Someone should be responsible for flowers, perhaps a relative, friend or member of the meeting. It may be helpful for someone to record ministry for the deaf or absent, and for another either to sit with someone unable to be present through infirmity or disability, or to visit afterwards to describe the funeral.

6.6 Children may wish to attend all or part of the meeting for worship and funeral. Elders should ensure that, as far as possible, the young are given full information and helped to prepare for the event (see *Quaker faith & practice* 12.12.i). One or more Friends should be ready to respond to their needs, as parents and carers may be too occupied with their own grieving and the business of the funeral. A creche or other childcare should be offered.

6.7 Refreshments may be offered after a funeral. The location used, the nature of the invitation, the provider of the refreshments, and the arrangements for payment should be clarified by the funeral coordinator.

6.8 Finally, it is sensible to nominate and brief a substitute in case of the funeral coordinator's sudden indisposition.

7 - DUTIES ON THE DAY

7.1 Following a cremation the next of kin may wish to receive the ashes; it is possible that the funeral coordinator may be asked to scatter the ashes at a later time. If so, the coordinator should check if any permission from the landowner is needed; also the wind direction at the time. The ashes should be in a container suitable for scattering. This can be provided by the crematorium, often in the form of an upright plastic urn. Caskets are more suitable for a burial.

7.2 If the preliminary planning has been comprehensive the funeral coordinator should otherwise have a straightforward programme on the day of the funeral. The coordinator should arrive early (wearing a reliable watch) and, where a meeting house is involved, check that the doors are open, that the heating is on if needed, and that the loop-system is operative. The coordinator should then check that all the relevant papers, leaflets, readings and any programmed elements are to hand.

7.3 As people arrive the funeral coordinator should check that the helpers are present, should greet arrivals, particularly non-Quakers and, if necessary, ensure that the bereaved are cared for.

7.4 The funeral coordinator may have no special part to play in the meeting for worship, where the appointed elders take the lead, nor at any subsequent refreshments, which may have been organised by a refreshments committee. The coordinator should concentrate on not fussing and should trust to the efficiency of those to whom the various tasks have been delegated.

7.5 The Friend who introduces the meeting for worship will devise the appropriate wording, bearing in mind the advice given in *Quaker faith &*

practice 17.01-06, the needs of those unfamiliar with a Quaker meeting, and the circumstances and personality of the deceased (see the following pages). It is important that everyone knows what to expect at each stage and that any young people and non-Quakers know that they can minister if they so wish.

8 - INTRODUCING AND CLOSING THE MEETING

8. The Committee on Eldership & Oversight has received a number of suggestions from individuals and meetings covering the main points to be included in an introduction and closing to the meeting for worship, and some phrases that have proved effective in practice. The following extracts may be adapted, or may prompt other ways of introducing and closing.

> Welcome, and thank you all for joining us today. This funeral is to be held in the manner of a Quaker meeting for worship; this means there is no appointed minister and no set order of service. During the meeting it is open for anyone to speak who feels moved to do so; such ministry is helpful and to be welcomed. It is best if contributions are brief and time allowed for reflection between them. Even without speaking what we can all bring to this occasion is our presence in a loving and sympathetic spirit. Towards the end the curtains will be drawn and there will follow a further short period of silent worship before the meeting is concluded by the shaking of hands. Let us now gather in a spirit of quiet trust and dependence on God, to pray together, to uphold one another, to share our sadness but more especially to celebrate and give thanks for the life of AB (or for the grace of God as shown in the life of AB).
>
> All who are gathered together here are asked to enter into the silent communion of prayer.
>
> There is no minister to lead us with set form of words, but God is present in this place, and God will listen to each one of us and will hear our prayers, whether they be spoken or silent.
>
> Let us remember with love and deep thankfulness the life of the friend whose spirit has just passed from this earth. Let us think of the source from which the goodness of that life was drawn - the love

of God, which unites in one fellowship the living and the dead.

Friends, we are gathered to remember our Friend...

We shall do this in the manner customary to Quakers...

There will be silence. Then, out of the stillness, any who feel led may stand and speak, remembering that there may be others who also have their message to impart.

If you are not familiar with this form of worship, do not feel discouraged from saying what is in your heart to say - for all are equal in the sight of God.

Some members of her/his family of whom she/he was very fond and to whom she/he was very dear are unable to be with us today. They will be with us in spirit and we shall remember them especially in our prayers... (mention by name)

The meeting will close after about .... minutes with the shaking of hands, and the curtains will be drawn across.

We have found the following Celtic blessing useful as a closing prayer where the deceased has had a troubled life and/or a distressing illness, and also where the family and friends present hold a variety of religious forms of belief.

Deep peace of the running wave to you;
Deep peace of the flowing air to you;
Deep peace of the quiet earth to you;
Deep peace of the shining stars to you;
Deep peace of the Son of Peace to you.

And so death has come to our Friend. His/Her hopes and ideals we commit into our minds and wills; his/her loves we commit into our hearts; his/her spirit has long been abroad in the world. We commit his/her body to its natural end.

9 - TASKS AFTERWARDS

9.1 After the proceedings are over the funeral coordinator has a number of routine tasks to perform. The death should be entered in monthly meeting records and noted for the revised list of members; it should also be included in any records associated with the burial ground. The Yearly Meeting offices should be notified in case the deceased was on any national committee, if possible enclosing a list of those committees, and any envelope labels, which normally have the code of the relevant mailing list. The funeral coordinator should also help with the circulation of personal leaflets to people unable to attend, and be prepared to help the next of kin, if desired, manage the settling of any expenses and with the details of any burial stones.

9.2 The needs of the bereaved will continue to be in the minds of overseers and other Friends in the weeks and months after the death, see especially sections 22.80-95 of *Quaker faith & practice*. Some may wish for privacy in their grief, but may well value continued contact with members of the meeting by visit, letter or telephone. Others may not want to be left alone, and some may need company but find it difficult to reach out. Friends will try to be sensitive to different or changing needs. If necessary, however, bereavement counselling should be arranged (see 'Organisations', page 32), while further practical help may be welcomed in a variety of matters. These include help in placing and paying for an announcement in *The Friend*, disposal of possessions and help with transport. The bereaved may also value help in claiming or changing state and occupational pensions, bank accounts, building society accounts, covenants and subscriptions, in paying bills and in notifying membership organisations especially if the deceased has held office in them. Then the bereaved may wish to acknowledge letters of condolence, but may be overwhelmed if these run into hundreds and may welcome an offer of help, at least by addressing envelopes.

9.3 Overseers need also to be alert to possible financial difficulties. These may be most acute in the months until probate is granted. When changes in income take effect the bereaved may need some time to adjust to the new financial regime, and tactful support may be welcomed.

9.4 Death brings grief, bewilderment, anxiety and even perhaps anger to those who are bereaved. These feelings are not short lived, and may indeed increase as time passes: the young may be particularly vulnerable. The first response of a meeting must be to provide sensitive care and support from those best able to offer it, in the belief that a loving sharing of these mixed feelings will bring healing in time. It is a duty of oversight to ensure that this help is being provided and continues for as long as it is needed.

10 - THE DIRECT EXPERIENCE OF FRIENDS AND MEETINGS

10.1 The following paragraphs are direct extracts from contributions sent by many meetings. Some are taken from the notes of guidance used by local funeral coordinators. Others are from leaflets or minutes addressed to members and attenders. Some Friends have written of their own personal experience. These accounts and insights are included here in the hope that they will be of help to readers. They are given without attribution, and verbatim except for very minor editorial changes to allow for consistency of presentation.

10.2 'It is of primary importance that the next of kin and close friends of the deceased are aware of the loving, thoughtful, and caring support of the meeting. The coordinator, and others who have contact with them, should seek to convey our desire to discern and to carry out their wishes to the best of our ability. At the same time, it is the elders (through the coordinator) who have experience in the conduct of Quaker funerals and it is their duty to guide the family to a choice that will be most satisfactory, both for them and for the rest of the meeting.'

10.3 'A funeral is an important event for us all, as it reminds us that death is part of life and we ourselves will die some day. It is not necessarily a sad occasion. For instance when death comes to someone who has had a long and fulfilled life, we can readily give thanks for that life. But death always means loss and for that we grieve - and need to grieve - so that in the process our feelings of loss and personal deprivation can become thankfulness for a life well-lived and our more negative (and inevitable) feelings of irritation with that person in life become mellowed into acceptance of her or his imperfections, and our own guilt at not having done more becomes something which can be forgiven. So a funeral is for the benefit of the living, and can be a deep spiritual experience. It is with this in mind that we need to get the practical details right.'

('The Direct Experience of Friends and Meetings' is continued on page 20)

Those filling in this form could consult their partner or spouse, cl
responsible for decisions about the funeral. Copies should be lod

Funerals and memorial meetings -

1. Name..

2. Address..

....

....

3. Phone ....

4. Member/attender of ....

....Quaker Meeting

5. Address..

....

....

(If the address is not known, contact Friends House, see page 32)

6. Next of kin or whoever would be responsible for decisions after your death

Name..

7. Address..

....

....

....

8. Executor's name......................................

9. Phone..

10. Address..

....

....

11. Solicitor's name

....

12. Phone..

13. Address..

....

....

14. Where is your will located? (please give full name and address, if not one of the above).

Name..

15. Address..

....

....

16. Phone..

relatives or friends, or other appropriate people, whoever would be with them, and with the funeral coordinators in the Quaker meeting.

Information and guidance in advance

How would you like your body to be disposed of?

- Cremation ☐
- Burial ☐
- Green burial ☐
- Medical Research (if so, give second choice) ☐
- Other (please specify) ☐

Any special wishes for disposal of ashes or burial of body

Would you like a Quaker burial/ disposal of ashes?

Yes ☐ No ☐

Where would you want a meeting for worship to be held, and when?

- meeting house ☐
- crematorium or cemetery chapel ☐
- private (please specify) ☐
- elsewhere ☐

21. Should death notices be published?

In *The Friend* ☐

Elsewhere (please specify) ☐

22. Who should be notified personally? Please attach a list, with addresses, or say where to find the information.

23. Do you wish for flowers?

Yes ☐   No ☐

24. Do you wish for gifts to charity?

Yes ☐   No ☐

Please specify:

25. Would you want a memorial meeting later, and if so where?

Yes ☐

No ☐

Signed..

Date..

10.4 'A funeral is for the benefit of the deceased, family and relations, Quakers, friends, or for strangers.'

10.5 'The funeral provides a dignified occasion for the disposal of human remains and underlines the importance of our bodies in life as well as in death. It provides a ritual no matter how simple it may be; this is of importance to most people irrespective of their religious belief or lack of belief. It provides some solace, comfort and perhaps hope to those close to the deceased. It is an opportunity for Friends and friends to remember and give thanks to the Lord for the grace shown forth in the life of the departed. It is a witness or testimony of Quaker faith and trustfulness to non-Quakers.'

10.6 'We should attempt to ensure that our funeral arrangements match up to our spiritual needs at the time of bereavement.'

10.7 'No two occasions are ever alike. We have known a large chapel and its gallery to be filled, with people sitting in the aisle and even in the sanctuary around the coffin, and the doors open with others listening from outside... and we have 'kept a meeting', just the two of us, to say farewell to a body that has been used for three years by a university department for research. The majority are small gatherings of kind, sympathetic people who are invariably appreciative of our small services. We find it a gentle and rewarding office to perform for Friends: especially as we are confident that the deceased Friend will probably be with us in spirit at the time.'

10.8 'We have recently had the funeral of a stillborn child. Panic-stricken, I asked one of the local clergy for help (thank goodness for good ecumenical relationships!) and though the prayers sent needed some modification there was enough to start the paralysed brain working. We found it was important in this case to refer at all times to the child by name and to bear in mind her potential which we felt was not lost though we could not see it develop.'

10.9 'There has been a problem when Humanists and others with no religious practice or faith (as far as one knows) request Quaker funerals, perhaps thinking that our silent meetings and lack of liturgy mean we are non-religious. Some preparative meetings have agreed to this request. In other meetings elders have tried to make sure the whole monthly meeting is aware that a funeral is a meeting for worship and part of our spiritual heritage. We have established friendly relations with the local Humanist group and now recommend referral to them when a non-religious funeral is sought.'

10.10 'Sometimes the person enquiring does want a religious funeral of some kind, though the deceased did not attend a meeting, or indeed any church. For example, 'my father went to a Quaker school, where he was very happy, and then he was a conscientious objector'; 'my sister subscribed to *Quaker monthly*, and always said she'd be a Quaker if she'd lived here'. A meeting for worship can then be the right kind of funeral, though great care is needed in preparation, and sensitivity in helping the bereaved understand what we can offer, and what we cannot. It is not an opportunity for Outreach!'

10.11 'All meetings are different and we must assess the kind of people likely to be present and the likely spirit in the meeting. After all there may be a large non-Quaker presence.'

10.12 'Quaker funerals are meetings for worship, based on waiting in the Spirit. We tend to think of ministry as spoken words, but ministry can be also be in music, in flowers, in movements and actions... The silence is the foundation of the worship, not a form.'

10.13 'Some meetings agree guidelines and stress the importance of silence. However music is permitted in moderation. In one case that meant very modern pop music which did not seem out of place for a burial of a young man with such interests who had loving and very genuine friends.'

10.14 'The value of vocal prayer at a funeral can hardly be over-emphasised. If offered under guidance it will often touch hearts too much distressed to listen to an address and will bring real comfort. This is above all to be borne in mind where there is some special ground for sorrow, when the anxious mourners may thus be helped to open their hearts to the healing stream of the divine love.'

10.15 'At a recent funeral, the minister had prepared the service very thoroughly. She was aware of problems within the family, and at the crematorium gathering, attended by just a few after the large public service, she said, 'If any of you have regrets about anything you have said, or that you meant to say and didn't, if you have any unfinished business, then take a few minutes to think of it now, and then recognise that this is the time to lay it down for ever.' I would like to feel that we could help Friends to handle situations of that kind, since the funeral provides a unique opportunity to take leave in more senses than one.'

10.16 'The absence of the body of the deceased at a memorial meeting combined with, usually, a greater period of time between the death and the meeting makes the occasion emotionally easier than a funeral for the family and close friends. What might be called 'words of comfort ministry' at funerals are much less common - and perhaps less acceptable - at memorial meetings. Ministry tends to come only from among those who knew the deceased. The meeting ends with the appointed elders shaking hands. It is appropriate for such meetings to be well publicised; many Friends will have been active and known in a variety of fields and the presence and ministry of persons from this wider circle and their ministry can add fresh insights, while also being helpful to them.'

10.17 'At one funeral, a young man commented 'Lots of flowers and no coffin - how nice', after such an arrangement.'

10.18 'We believe in the Society as a community - it is the Religious Society of Friends - and therefore it is fitting to attend the meeting for worship, to remember, to give thanks and to take leave of Friends who have died. It is the last service we can offer, a tribute of respect, and it matters to the group (the preparative meeting) as it is a service to them too, for it strengthens them; see *Quaker faith & practice* 17.04. There is also need for the presence of others and their attendance in a loving and sympathetic spirit is a very real ministry.'

10.19 'As I am notorious for my view that ministry should only be given when one finds oneself giving it, perhaps my exhortations that weddings and funerals are the only occasions where it is one's duty to come prepared to minister, even if the preparations remain in pocket or handbag if not needed, have more weight. Because we are in a holiday and retirement area it does happen that we are called on for the funeral of a Friend whom we do not know. On these occasions I have found that Friends rally round, and posting reliable people ready primed can save the situation. I salve my conscience by reminding myself that the deceased would understand and my prime concern must be the family.'

10.20 'A teacher helped a child with learning difficulties prepare for his mother's funeral: they talked about her suicide, about life, and death, and love; what happens at a funeral; and how he felt about his mother and his own loss. And then, at the meeting, the teacher read a poem chosen by the child, with the child's own introductory words. If only we could all be given such sensitive help in preparing ourselves! How can we help those who might have difficulty speaking, through emotion, or disability, or some other inhibition?'

10.21 'We have found it best if the elder who is introducing confines his or her remarks to a description of what is to happen, while a second elder is ready with an agreed reading or other ministry after a suitable break. If the introducing elder does both, there may be a long gap afterwards. This does not matter in itself, but spoken ministry may then start uncomfortably close to the time at which we are required to finish.'

10.22 'Acting as a funeral coordinator does make demands on your emotional core which might come as a surprise, so you need to have thought about it, to have participated earlier in a minor capacity, and to have some sort of guidelines to follow.'

10.23 'Obviously, by my age I have experienced a number of deaths of relatives and close friends, and during that time my feeling towards the final ceremony has changed from personal private sorrow to the feeling that this is the last thing I can do for the person who has died - a tribute of respect, a feeling of solidarity with other friends present. It is also something I can and need to do for myself, that is to recognise that the familiar presence is no longer there, and that I go on without the external support, but with the knowledge of that person's influence and what it has meant to me over the years. In this respect, my mother's funeral was the catalyst. I didn't go to it, because I had just been married and was living in Hong Kong, and she died in England. Furthermore, she hadn't been expected to die, and she had just spent six months with us. But I've always wished I had been able to be there, and since then, for people I've had a special relationship with, I've always tried to go to their funeral.'

10.24 'When we turn to *Quaker faith & practice* 12.12.f, we read that one of the duties of elders is to take responsibility for the right holding of meetings for worship on special occasions such as funerals. In this monthly meeting we are all elders, and, accepting this responsibility, we should read through carefully chapters 12, 17 and 22 of *Quaker faith &*

practice, and note that we are authorised to hold meetings for worship on the occasion of a death - either at the crematorium, or at a burial in our burial ground, or at a memorial meeting, usually at a later date.'

10.25 'The person appointed as funeral coordinator may not feel able to or wish to arrange a particular funeral or memorial meeting for a variety of reasons which may include: just wishing to be a mourner, feeling too affected by the death, being unhappy about the relationships with the family or the deceased, having been recently bereaved themselves. It must always be easy to ask somebody else to be responsible.'

Table 1 - Preliminary planning

TO CONSIDER	TO DECIDE
disposal of body	decide on method
preferred place, date and time of disposal	decide whether choices are practicable, and if so obtain agreement of responsible authorities
attendance	decide whether funeral is to be limited by invitation, or to immediate family and friends, or open to all; decide if funeral is to be a meeting for worship under the care of the meeting, or a ceremony arranged by the next of kin with the support and help of individual Quakers
likely numbers and any special needs	decide whether numbers can be accommodated and whether special needs can be met
flowers	decide whether there are to be flowers, wreaths, etc.
programmed readings and music	decide whether these are thought desirable
leaflet of remembrance	decide whether one is to be produced, and if it is needed before the funeral; if so decide on author, and obtain the author's agreement
preferred location and timing of meeting for worship	decide when and where any meeting for worship should be held (if separate from, or in addition to, the funeral)

(continued overleaf)

refreshments	decide whether there are to be refreshments afterwards, where, who is to organise, who is to pay
later memorial meeting	decide on preferred date, time and place of a later memorial meeting (if wished); confirm practicability
notices of death, funeral, etc.	decide on content and placing of these in press, who pays; also mailing of personal letters or telephone calls, and who is responsible

Table 2 - Detailed planning

at Quaker burial ground	confirm location, date and time; contact the reponsible person listed in the local book of members and/or MM elders to find local procedures and obtain permission
at crematorium or cemetery	contact staff; find out local procedures governing order of arrivals, closing of curtains/lowering of coffin, digging a grave, music, departures, etc; modify seating if necessary, by agreement; remove or cover undesirable religious symbols if possible; brief all staff on Quaker ways; agree timings
meeting for worship	confirm location, date and time; arrange for elders, doorkeepers, etc. to be present; check availability of any needed programmed items; arrange distribution of leaflets; appoint deputies
access to all above	check public transport, travel by car, parking, toilets, wheelchair access, temporary seating, shelter from rain or sun

PUBLICATIONS

Although this booklet focuses on funerals and memorial meetings, this resources list ranges wider, and includes caring for the dying, facing our own mortality, readings, theology, grief, and caring for those who are grieving. Insights from other Christian churches and other faiths are included, for their experience can illuminate ours. Most of the books list other relevant publications and also helpful organisations.

Those responsible for oversight and eldership may wish to direct the bereaved to some items on the list and indeed to read the books themselves.

If a meeting intends to buy one of the books, its availability, price and postage should be checked with the Quaker Bookshop. The Bookshop can take orders by post, telephone, fax or e-mail. Some of the books can be borrowed from the Quaker Home Service Resources Room. Please telephone the central offices for details (see Britain Yearly Meeting, 'Organisations' page 32).

Some preparative meetings may not have a library nor be able to buy many publications. In such cases monthly meeting might consider how to share materials on eldership and oversight and make publications speedily available, possibly by cataloguing on a monthly meeting basis.

Quaker faith & practice The book of Christian discipline of the Yearly Meeting of the Religious Society of Friends (Quakers) in Britain 1994
Essential reading, especially chapters 12, 17 and 22.

Quaker funerals Quaker Home Service, single A5 leaflet
A short, explanatory leaflet, which could be mailed with the notice of the funeral or given to worshippers at the funeral.

Charter for the bereaved Institute of Burial and Cremation Administration, available to purchase from IBCA, see 'Organisations' below.
Based on the experiences of cemetery and crematorium managers with bereaved families: sets out standards of service, rights of the bereaved and others involved, aiming to give the bereaved greater influence over funeral arrangements, thereby controlling costs and offering more satisfaction.

Abrams, Rebecca *When parents die* Charles Letts & Co 1992
'Written for people like me, whose parents have died': the time immediately following, different kinds of death, difficult grieving (including problems with eating, drugs, alcohol), letting go of grief without abandoning your memories, or being afraid to remember.

Albery, Editor *New natural death handbook* Rider 1997 (£11.65 including postage and packing from the Natural Death Centre, see 'Organisations' page 32)
A comprehensive and practical handbook, that includes deeply moving personal accounts; looking after someone dying at home; how to organise a funeral without an undertaker; writing a living will, advance funeral wishes form and death plan; descriptions of all the woodland burial grounds in the UK; Good Funeral Guide to the best undertakers; cardboard and conventional coffins by mail order.

Albery, Irvine, Buckley, Pieau, Editors, *Creative endings: Designer Dying & Celebratory Funerals*, Natural Death Centre 1996
The 1996 collection of projects, ideas, articles, resources, including a discussion on fasting (in contrast to intrusive medical care or active euthanasia).

Albery, Irvine, Evans, Editors, *Sooner or later: Preparing for Dying and Family-Organised Funerals*, Natural Death Centre 1997
The 1997 collection of ideas and articles sent in to the Centre, including the dos and don'ts of grieving, funeral rip-offs, suggestions for preparing for dying.

Albery, Mezey, McHugh, Papworth, Editors *Before and after: The best new ideas for improving the quality of dying and for inexpensive, green, family-organised funerals*, Natural Death Centre 1995
The 1995 collection of information, resources, including dying at home, green do-it-yourself funerals.

Chapman, Christine *In love abiding: Responding to the Dying and Bereaved*, SPCK 1995
A reflective book, with chapters on stillbirth, children, teenagers; considers forgiving those who have caused death; includes a prayer at each chapter end. 'Nobody ever really knows how another person feels, but you can learn to listen and find out. You can be alongside, you can love and support, confident in the knowledge that it does not matter what you hope to achieve, but what Christ can achieve through you.'

Dominica, Sister Frances *Just my reflection: Helping parents to do things their way when their child dies*, Darton, Longman & Todd 1997
Written out of the experience of a hospice for children: includes practical ways for the bereaved family to exercise choices at the time of death, and find comfort in expressing love for their child to the very last. The first section offers advice on the various decisions that will have to be made, the options open to the family and the legal requirements. The second section is an anthology of readings, songs and prayers (Christian and other) from which the family may create a funeral service which is fitting for their child.

Durston, David *Growing through grief: Sharing Our Experience of Loss*, Bible Society 1991
Six-session course to help groups tackle some issues, share feelings, reflecting on members' personal experience, exploring biblical situations and passages, in order to discover new insights. Not a professional training course, but useful preparation for Friends appointed for funerals, or for a pastoral care circle or study group open to this deep topic.

Gill, Sue and Fox, John *The dead good funerals book* Engineers of the Imagination 1996, revised 1997
Organising your own non-religious or alternative ceremony, and much practical information (e.g. simple coffin design, resource lists). Robust and refreshing in its criticism of some conventional funerals.

Hollins, Sheila and Sireling, Lester *When dad died* Silent Books 1989
A simply written picture book for children, or adults with learning difficulties; better to learn about death before coming face to face, but also helpful in thinking back to a loss; the pain of grieving, saying goodbye, remembering Dad who died of an illness and was cremated. In a companion volume, Mum was buried.

Illingworth, Mary *How to direct your own funeral*, Independent Funeral Advisory Service, PO Box 1, Watchet, Somerset, TA23 0AX

Jewett, Claudia *Helping children cope with separation & loss*, Batsford 1984, Clear and practical guidance for social workers, therapists, counsellors, parents and friends. Loss by death, but also by divorce, abandonment; making sense of it all; good chapter on telling a child; useful information on developmental stages.

Krementz, Jill *How it feels when a parent dies* Victor Gollancz 1983, 1986
Children, aged 7-16 years, talk simply of their parents' deaths (by accident, illness, suicide), their grieving, the help they appreciated, life since, step-parents, remembering, the kinds of people they (the children) are now. One of the most helpful books for the young to read for themselves, whether they or a friend or classmate is bereaved.

Kübler-Ross, Elisabeth *On children and death* Macmillan 1983
Drawn from deep experience with dying children, this is one of the first and best on this subject. Particularly good on talking with children: the author believes that they know what the outcome of their illness will be, and want to talk. Also considers young friends and family, being present in the dying, saying goodbye in one's own way.

Lampen, Diana *Facing death* (QHS 1979) Imprint Systems, Wanganui, NZ 1996
William Penn wrote that 'we cannot love to live if we cannot bear to die'. Diana Lampen emphasises practical ways of overcoming our natural fear, and the grief we experience through the death of others. She draws on many people's experience, illuminated throughout by her own awareness of the love of God. A basic book for Quaker meetings.

Saunders, Cicely *Beyond the horizon: A Search for Meaning in Suffering* Darton, Longman & Todd 1990
An anthology of pieces from well-known authors and Dame Cicely's hospice patients. 'Why?' is answered by a sense of the sharing of God in all our losses; by asking instead 'How?' we can see the growth in the heart of pain.

Snell, Beatrice Saxon *Horizon*, FHSC 1972
An anthology of Quaker, Biblical and other readings, particularly suitable for Quaker funerals and memorial meetings

Taylor, Allegra *Acquainted with the night: A year on the frontiers of death* The CW Daniel Company 1995
The story of a year working in a hospice: death is not the enemy, it is possible to 'be there' for someone dying or bereaved, to grieve well and to die well ourselves.

Wells, Rosemary *Helping children cope with grief: Facing a death in the family* SPCK 1988
There is a great deal that a caring adult - parent, teacher, nurse, neighbour, friend - can do to avoid the long-term distress which can be caused by hidden fears and anxieties. A straightforward, simply written but sensitive book.

Whitaker, Agnes *All in the end is harvest* Darton Longman & Todd 1984, 1996.
A bedside book, a source of readings for funerals, food for thought and for strengthening, a collection of contributions (religious and from other sources) from counsellors and members of Cruse Bereavement Care: one of the best of such anthologies.

Wilcock, Penelope *Spiritual care of Dying and Bereaved People*, SPCK 1996
'In confronting the business of dying, which all of us have to face, we are not talking about turning our backs on life, we are daring to be led into the very heart of living.' Written out of experience as a hospice chaplain, practical and honest, prayerful yet with a deep understanding for those of other faiths or no religion at all (a good model of how to relate to people who think and feel differently from yourself, whatever the focus).

Planning for those you leave behind Cruse Bereavement Care (see 'Organisations' page 32 for address, to ask for full publications list)
A useful Cruse booklet about making a will, inheritance tax, funeral plans, and other practical matters.

What to do when someone dies Which? Ltd 1997
Legal requirements for the whole of the UK and abroad, claiming benefits, arranging funeral yourself, how the funerals ombudsman scheme works, lists of resources, written in a practical and sympathetic style. Regularly updated, check for latest edition.

Wills and probate Which? Ltd 1997
Guidance on how to write your own will, with or without a solicitor, complex legal and tax concepts, how to secure probate without using a solicitor, draft letters to help administer an estate; describes law and procedures for England and Wales, with outline of main differences applying in Scotland and Northern Ireland. Regularly updated, check for latest edition.

ORGANISATIONS

The following organisations are listed as a starting point - they all offer a variety of services and publications, and could refer you on to local branches and to dozens of other organisations. It would be helpful to collect some information before there is an immediate need. In particular, the meeting's funeral coordinator could have available up-to-date information such as addresses of funeral directors familiar with Quaker ways, lists of charges and other relevant local details.

BRITAIN YEARLY MEETING, Friends House, 173/177 Euston Road, London NW1 2BJ, telephone 0171 663 1000; Fax: 0171 663 1001; Web: http://www.quaker.org.uk; Bookshop direct line: 0171 663 1030
Relevant information and support are available from the central offices. The Quaker Bookshop publishes a catalogue of publications from all Quaker publishers worldwide, takes orders in person, by phone, fax, e-mail or post. In Quaker Home Service department, the Resources Room lends books and study material (for adults and children); the Committee on Eldership & Oversight and Children & Young People's Committee offer training and publications, and can be consulted on specific matters. A leaflet containing brief details and contact addresses of over thirty independent Quaker-run accommodation schemes for elderly people is available free from the Secretary to the Quaker Housing Trust.

THE COMPASSIONATE FRIENDS 53 North Street, Bristol, BS3 1EN. Office telephone/fax: 0117 966 5202; help line: 0117 953 9639
A nationwide organisation of bereaved parents, offering friendship and understanding to other bereaved parents, with links around the world.

CRUSE BEREAVEMENT CARE 126 Sheen Road, Richmond, Surrey TW9 1UR. Telephone: 0181 940 4818, bereavement line: 0181 322 7227 weekdays 9.30 am - 5.00 pm.
A registered charity offering counselling, information and, where possible, social support through nearly 200 local branches throughout the UK. Their comprehensive publications list includes books and leaflets (some free) about bereavement, losing a partner, practical information, comforting the bereaved, help for bereaved children, schools, people with learning disabilities, counselling, research and professional journals.

INSTITUTE OF BURIAL AND CREMATION ADMINISTRATION, 1 The Terrace, City of London Cemetery, Manor Park, London E12 5D. Tel/fax: 0181 989 9496
See *Charter for the Bereaved*, page 27.

LESBIAN & GAY BEREAVEMENT PROJECT Vaughan M Williams Centre, Colindale Hospital, London NW9 5HG, Helpline telephone 0181 455 8894 7pm - 12pm daily.
To support lesbians and gay men who have lost a partner, to advise on the importance of writing wills, and to educate the helping professions about lesbian and gay bereavement.

MUNICIPAL OR PRIVATE CEMETERY OR CREMATORIUM: find them in the phone book. Municipal facilities are usually listed under the local council. Contact the Institute of Burial and Cremation (IBCA) listed above if you require the telephone number, address, etc. of local members.
Contact the supervisor of the local crematorium or cemetery to arrange a visit, find out about the services they offer, attend an open day, ask for leaflets. For example, the City of Carlisle Bereavement Services at the cemetery office offer the following free handouts: Woodland burial, Environmental issues, Guide to independent burial, Questions people ask about cremation, Guide to independent cremation, Cremation memorial facilities, Information on using a funeral director, Guiding principles for burial & cremation services, Copy of funeral directive to go with will, Charter for the bereaved, Biodegradable coffins and shroud, Copy of living will, Table of fees, Details from Natural Death Centre, Laying out and caring for the deceased, Plans of cemeteries & gardens, Outline of a secular service, Information on embalming, Regulations.

NATURAL DEATH CENTRE 20 Heber Road, London NW2 6AA.
Telephone 0181 208 2853, fax: 0181 452 6434.
E-mail: rhino@dial.pipex.com
Website: www.newciv.org/GIB/naturaldeath.html
An educational charity that provides a Befriending Network where trained volunteers visit the homes of those who are dying, to sit with the person or to relieve the carer; it also provides information on inexpensive, environmentally-friendly, family-organised funerals and runs the Association of Nature Reserve Burial Grounds for the 75+ woodland burial grounds in the UK, where cardboard coffins are used and a tree planted instead of having a headstone. Their main information resource is their comprehensive handbook - recommended for funeral coordinators' libraries.

NATIONAL ASSOCIATION OF FUNERAL DIRECTORS, 618 Warwick Road, Solihull, West Midlands, B91 1AA, telephone 0121 711 1343
The Code of Practice sets out their principles, including general conduct, advertising, information, basic funeral, estimates, confirmations and invoices, professional conduct, complaints, etc.

SOCIETY OF ALLIED AND INDEPENDENT FUNERAL DIRECTORS, Crowndale House, 1 Ferdinand Place, Camden, London NW1 8EE, Telephone 0171 267 6777, Fax: 0171-267 1147 Internet: http//www.saif.org.uk   e-mail: infor@saif.org.uk
Code of practice, which includes maintenance of client confidentiality, display of charges, provision of simple funerals.

LOCAL NAMES, ADDRESSES AND TELEPHONE NUMBERS

FOR YOUR MEETING'S NOTES